MW01115589

TAKE ME BACK TO ITALY

GEOGRAPHY EDUCATION FOR KIDS

CHILDREN'S EXPLORE THE WORLD BOOKS

BABY PROFESSOR
EDUCATION KIDS

Speedy Publishing LLC

40 E. Main St. #1156

Newark, DE 19711

www.speedypublishing.com

Copyright 2017

Italy

In this book, we're going to talk about
and explore the beautiful country of Italy.
So, let's get right to it!

ITALY is located in the south-central region of Europe and has some of the most scenic landscapes on Earth. If you look at a map of the world, you'll see that the country of Italy looks something like a giant boot. Its landmass is about 300,000 square kilometers, which is a little larger than the state of Arizona. The islands of Sicily and Sardinia are also part of the country of Italy.

Tyrrhenian Sea in Italy

THE PENINSULA OF ITALY

Italy is a peninsula, which means it's bordered by water on three sides.

The three bodies of water that surround Italy are:

- The Tyrrhenian Sea to Italy's west
- The Adriatic Sea to Italy's east
- The Mediterranean Sea to the west and southwest

If you're visiting the northern part of Italy, you can easily travel to four different countries. The countries of France and Switzerland are an easy drive to the northwest and the countries of Austria and Slovenia are an easy drive to the northeast.

Innsbruck Cityscape, Austria

Gran Paradiso National Park, Italy

MOUNTAINS AND VOLCANOES

About 40% of Italy is mountainous. The majestic Alps Mountains span the top of Italy. A famous mountain in the Italian Alps is Gran Paradiso, which has a height of 13,323 feet and is located in the Graian Alps. The Apennines Mountains form a "backbone" for the country. They connect at the western region of the Alps and stretch all the way down to the tip of the boot.

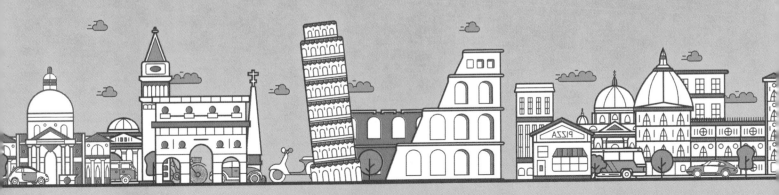

If you travel west of the Apennines, you will find the forested hills of Rome and other historic cities. In the southern part of the country, there are hot, sunny coastlands as well as plains with fertile soils where farmers grow olives and figs.

Harvesting Olives in Sicily Village, Italy

Mountain Etna, Sicily

Italy has the only volcanoes in mainland Europe that are active. Three of the volcanoes in Italy have erupted within the last century.

- Mount Etna on the island of Sicily
- Stromboli, located on the Aeolian Islands
- Mount Vesuvius, located near Naples

Mount Vesuvius last erupted in the year 1944 and is the only volcano on the mainland of the European continent that is active. Etna and Stromboli both have some continuous volcanic activity.

Mount Vesuvius View

Capodimonte on Bolsena Lake,
lazio, Italy

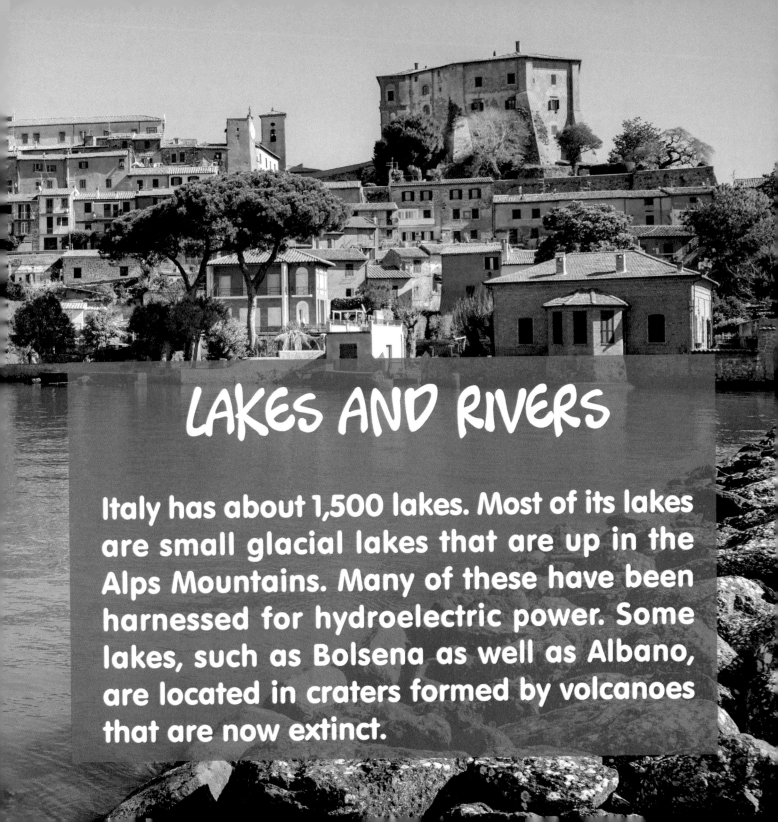

LAKES AND RIVERS

Italy has about 1,500 lakes. Most of its lakes are small glacial lakes that are up in the Alps Mountains. Many of these have been harnessed for hydroelectric power. Some lakes, such as Bolsena as well as Albano, are located in craters formed by volcanoes that are now extinct.

Italy's largest lakes were cut into the foothills of the Alps by glaciers during the Quaternary period, which began 2.5 million years ago. The three largest of these Alpine lakes are Lake Garda, Lake Maggiore, and Lake Como. The most famous of these three lakes is Lake Como because many well-known celebrities have resort homes there.

Lake Como, Milan, Italy

Po River

The longest river in Italy is the Po and it travels east from its source in the Cottian Alps until it drains into the Adriatic Sea, a distance of about 400 miles. The basin of the river is important to the agricultural industry in northern Italy. The Adige is the second longest of Italy's rivers. It travels for 255 miles. Just like the Po River, it originates in the Alps, and eventually drains into the Adriatic. The river has very rapid currents and is used for both hydroelectric power as well as irrigation.

PLACES TO VISIT IN ITALY

ROME

Rome is Italy's capital city. Filled with amazing ancient architecture and hundreds of historic sites, Rome is one of the most interesting cities to explore in Italy. Some of the wonderful places to see include:

- The Colosseum, where gladiators fought in ancient times

Colosseum in Rome

Pantheon, Rome, Italy

- The Forum, where there are ruins of the incredible architecture built by the ancient Romans
- The Pantheon, where the ancient Romans worshipped their gods and goddesses and which has an enormous dome with a hole in its center

- **The Appian Way, which is one of the earliest Roman stone roads**
- **The Palatine Hill, which is the most famous and the centermost of Rome's seven hills**

Appia Antica in Rome

Basilica di San Pietro, Vatican, Rome, Italy

- **The Vatican, which is the center of the Roman Catholic Church and contains precious artwork collected over the centuries**
- **The Trevi Fountain, which is one of the most stunning fountains in the world with ancient statues and cascading water**

- **The Spanish Steps, which has 138 steps, is the widest set of steps in Europe, and is a wonderful place to walk and people watch**
- **The Borghese Gardens, which contain hundreds of acres of beautiful landscaping, museums, and a zoo**

It would take many weeks to see all that there is to see in Rome. Legend says that if you throw a coin in the Trevi Fountain, you'll come back to Rome someday.

Spanish Steps at Dusk, Rome, Italy

Canal in Venice, Italy

VENICE

Venice is a magical city that was built on the water. The gondolas are its main attraction. They are long, flat-bottomed boats that travel on the city's beautiful canal streets lined with colorful houses. The gondoliers are dressed in striped shirts and wear straw hats. As they row the gondolas, they take travelers up and down the Grand Canal and sometimes serenade them by singing opera songs.

FLORENCE

During the Renaissance period, the city of Florence was a center of art and culture. The massive dome of the Cathedral of Santa Maria del Fiore is a world- famous architectural structure. It took the architect Filippo Brunelleschi most of his life to complete. He had to create new ways to lift heavy supplies up into the dome and his innovations were used by later architects.

The Basilica di Santa Maria del Fiore

If you're not afraid of heights, you can climb up the 463 steps of the narrow workmen's passageways to the top of the dome to see a breathtaking vista of the city.

The museums of Florence are filled with priceless works of art, many of which were commissioned by the influential Medici family. They were the rulers of the city-state of Florence for 200 years and were patrons of the arts. They sponsored some of Italy's most famous painters and sculptors, including Michelangelo, Donatello, Raphael, and Leonardo da Vinci.

Leonardo Da Vinci

Galileo Galilei

There is a special museum devoted to Leonardo da Vinci's art and inventions. There's also a small museum that showcases the many inventions and scientific contributions made by the famous astronomer Galileo Galilei.

THE AMALFi COAST AND THE ISLAND OF CAPRI

The peninsula of Amalfi is located south of the city of Naples. The road to get there is narrow and steep, but the view of the expansive, blue Tyrrhenian Sea from there is spectacular.

Amalfi Coast

Capri Island

The houses and buildings are built on the city's steep slopes and flowers cover the hillsides. Off the peninsula is Capri, which is a famous island known for its sea cave called the Blue Grotto.

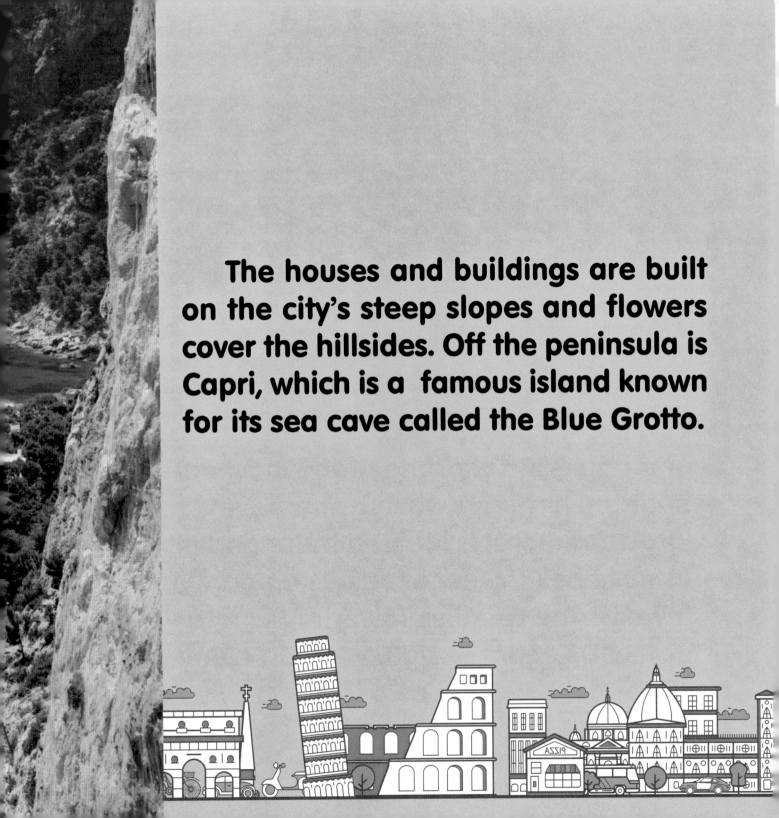

PISA

In the city of Pisa in Tuscany, Italy is the Campo dei Miracoli, which means the "field of miracles." It was one of the most ambitious building projects during medieval times. A large cathedral is located there and a world-famous bell tower called a "campanile." That tower is the Leaning Tower of Pisa. If you are at least 8 years of age, you can climb to the top of the tower to see a beautiful vista of the town.

Leaning tower of Pisa, Italy

Ruins of Pompeii, Italy

POMPEII

Mount Vesuvius, which is one of Italy's active volcanoes, erupted very suddenly in 79 AD. The nearby Roman city of Pompeii was encased in volcanic ash and many thousands died. In the 18th century, archaeologists began to excavate the ruins there and many amazing artifacts have been found.

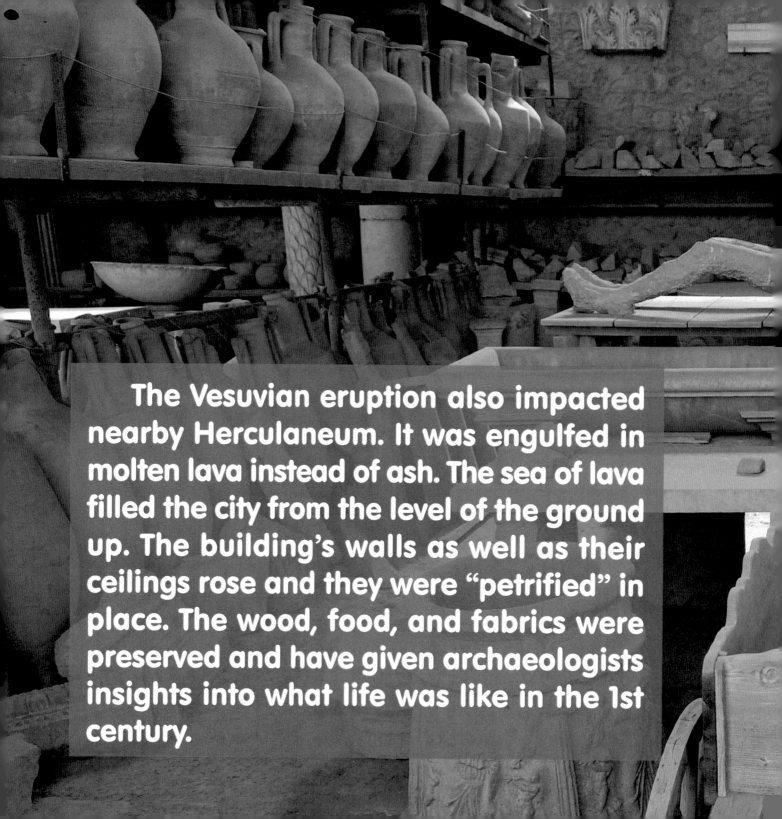

The Vesuvian eruption also impacted nearby Herculaneum. It was engulfed in molten lava instead of ash. The sea of lava filled the city from the level of the ground up. The building's walls as well as their ceilings rose and they were "petrified" in place. The wood, food, and fabrics were preserved and have given archaeologists insights into what life was like in the 1st century.

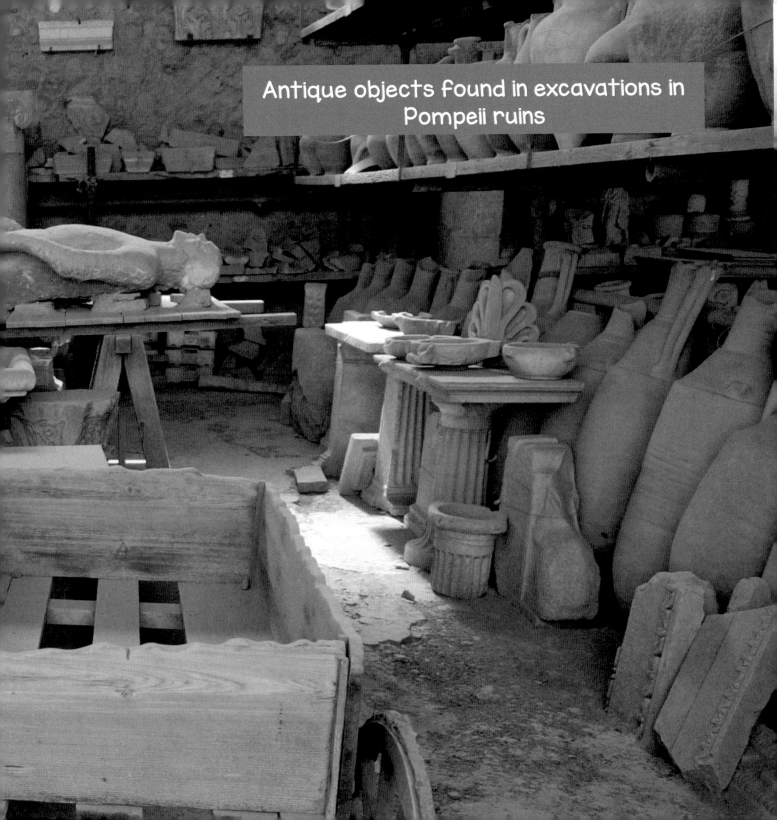

Antique objects found in excavations in Pompeii ruins

The Famous Temple of Concordia

SICILY

The island of Sicily is known for its amazing Greek temples that date to ancient times. In the city of Agrigento there is a Valley of Temples where you can see four well-preserved temples that the Greeks built to worship their gods and goddesses:

- **Tempio di Concordia, the best preserved of Sicily's Doric temples**
- **Tempio di Juno Lacinia**

- Tempio di Olympian Zeus, which was the largest of all four, but was partially destroyed by an earthquake
- Tempio di Heracles

Temple of Olympian Zeus, Athens, Greece

AMAZING ITALY

The country of Italy is in the south-central section of Europe. Surrounded by water on three sides, the coastlines of Italy have towns on steep cliffs and beautiful views of the water. The terrain in Italy is very mountainous. The Alps span the top of the country with their pristine glacial lakes. The Apennines run from the western edge of the Alps to the southern tip of the boot. The capital city of Rome, the canal city of Venice, and the Renaissance city of Florence are only three of the amazing cities in Italy that are filled with art, culture, and history. Throw a coin in Rome's Trevi Fountain so you're destined to come back.

Make a Wish!

Awesome! Now that you know more about the country of Italy you may want to find out more information about the Vatican City in the Baby Professor book The Holy See: A Kid's Guide to Exploring the Vatican City.

Visit

BABY PROFESSOR
EDUCATION KIDS

www.BabyProfessorBooks.com

to download Free Baby Professor eBooks
and view our catalog of new and exciting
Children's Books